IMB...

YOUNG Opine

Villains

WIRE PETRICHOR

NO

FOX PICNIC

HYPERNYM

DON'T
CALL IT
That

Second Edition

Front Matter

ExtraCurricular Press
327 Guerrero Street
San Francisco, CA 94103
extracurricularpress.com

First edition October 2013
Second edition November 2016

For Alex and Allie.

Say hello to the second edition of *Don't Call It That.* You might be asking yourself *"What's so special about the second edition?"* Well, I'll tell you what. There are six entirely new chapters covering subjects like *To Verb or Not to Verb, Words- mash,* and *The Power of Isolation.* There are five interview vignettes with people who have used *Don't Call It That* to name their businesses. The trademark section has been significantly expanded, including an interview with a real life intellectual property attorney. Four new name species have also been discovered.

Now with 40% more!

I, along with Brian Scott and ExtraCurricular Press, have partnered with Miguel Reyes and Commercial Type on all of the illustra- tion and typography in the second edition.

So please, put this book to good use and share what you come up with.

Contains:

1   Aim for the Eyes
2   You're Awful at This
3   Ready, Set
4   Get to the Point
5   Jumping Through Hoops
6   Make Some Headroom
7   The Attention Deficit
8   Show Don't Tell
9   Wordsmash
10   Kids, Dogs, Goldfish
11   I'm with Stupid
12   Don't Reinvent the Wheel
13   The Power of Isolation
14   New Species Discovered Daily
15   Push and Pull
16   Apples and Alligators
17   Love at First Sight
18   Names Are Living Beings
19   How to Ask Friends
20   Climbing Over Clichés
21   To Verb or Not to Verb
22   Field Exercise
23   The Proving Grounds

Aim for the Eyes
How names make our lives easier.

When you were in grade school, some librarian probably told you not to judge a book by its cover. Then he or she probably went on to tell you how you shouldn't judge people by their proverbial covers because we're all so complex and on and on. Seems like good enough advice, right?

The only problem is, everyone judges books by their covers.

The psychology behind this is pretty basic. We're constantly bombarded by tons of products, advertising, and marketing to the point where we're not mentally equipped to pay attention to everything that ends up in front of our two little eyes. Dr. Martin Hilbert of the University of California at Davis works on calculating the amount of information humans process. He estimates we're bombarded by the equivalent of 174 entire newspapers-worth of data every single day. This represents a fivefold increase since 1986.

If you had to catalog every brand you came upon in a single day, it would be an all-consuming task. The world is saturated with brands, and, as a result, advertisers get excited when two percent of the exposed audience responds actively—for example, clicking on an ad, retweeting, or like-ing a *Facebook* post.

The result is some mental triage. We subconsciously set up simple tests to take small amounts of surface-level information, like what a company is called and how it looks, in order to instantaneously decide whether it's worth paying attention to.

We pay attention to the content that catches our attention. It's a coping mechanism for the all-out marketing blitz we face every day of our lives.

If we didn't develop a way to figure out what's worth paying attention to, we'd spend months in the toothpaste aisle at the grocery store comparing anti-cavity claims and being mesmerized by foil packaging.

With such a small window to catch someone's attention, what you call yourself becomes important. This need is amplified for startups. They only have so much time to show people that they're gaining traction before funding dries up. It's hard to gain traction if people can't remember what you're called. The name is often the first thing anyone will come in contact with.

It's your first impression. Do you want your first impression with your audience to be something that's cool and interesting and helps you tell your story? Or do you want it to be something that sounds like everything else and gets ignored?

Since a name is a very compact, easy-to-communicate piece of information, a good name can grab people's attention instantly. A good name can make people want to learn more. It can also make people smile or laugh. When people say they get business through "word of mouth," what is actually being passed from person to person? The name.

To get you into the process of naming things, I've structured this book as a series of exercises. The exercises lead from one to the next. It's hands-on for a reason. There's a difference between studying art history and studying art. That is to say, this book isn't about the theory or philosophy behind naming. It's simply about the process of naming and how to come up with great names.

Heads Up

When I read through my first draft of this book, I realized that I had referred interchangeably to products, companies, and services. In most cases they all function similarly, and for clarity, in this final version of the book, I've called them all "brands."

You're Awful at This
Bad names are your best friend.

One of the things that frustrates me and that people don't appreciate is that there are so many bad movies. You have to have some feeling about how bad a movie can be before you can appreciate the good ones.

Andrew Sarris

Exercise 1

So let's start with something pretty simple. Write down the idea behind your brand in one sentence or phrase. Don't over think it. Maybe it's an upscale ice cream truck or intuitive video editing software or yoga for veterans. Whatever floats your boat.

Write down your main idea behind your brand in one sentence or phrase. If it doesn't come to you right away, try a few things and see what feels the most distinct.

Exercise 2

Now, come up with 15 or so really bad names for your project. If we're doing upscale ice cream, maybe something like:

iScream
Premium Ice Cream, Inc.
Cream of the Ice
Not Popsicles
Cold Cream
Milk Gone Bad
32 Flavors
Flavorz Extreme
Kolbalio

You get the picture.

Come up with 15 or so "bad" names.

1
2
3
4
5
6
7
8
9
10
11
12
13
14
15

We're starting with bad names for a few reasons. Primarily, it's a lot easier to think of bad stuff than good stuff. This is evidenced by how negative of a place the internet can be—get one reference wrong and you get flamed from all directions. Additionally, figuring out what makes names bad is a good place to start thinking about what makes names good. Flip the switch on the bad attributes of these names, and you start to get some qualities that you might want to focus on.

So let's look at why bad names are bad:

They're descriptive: Unless you're doing something truly compelling, having a name that describes what you do is a guaranteed way to make sure people never pay attention to you. An example I always like to use is the airline, *AirTran*. They do transportation... in the air...fascinating. Sure they might be a successful company, but their name is sleep-inducing and hard to remember, and says absolutely nothing about their point of view. Then again, *AirTran* has a good reason for a bland name—they needed to fly under the radar after ditching their previous name, *ValuJet*, following the 1996 crash. Think of a few descriptive names and write them down. It shouldn't be hard—they're a dime a dozen.

They try to encompass everything: A lot of people take the desire to not pigeonhole themselves way too far and avoid showing any personality whatsoever. Being overly general leads to boring names that have nothing to do with your specific proposition. This is why so many companies say they're in the "solutions business." Anything can be construed as a solution: *Waste Management Solutions, Business Intelligence Solutions, Container Solutions.* The point is, picking a name that 'doesn't rule anything out' generally doesn't draw anyone in either.

Exercise 3

Come up with 15 or so descriptive names for your project. Here are some examples:

AirTran
vitaminwater
Airbus
General Electric
Whole Foods
Grocery Outlet
General Motors
Bank of America
American Greetings
International Watch Company (IWC)

Write down some descriptive names.

1
2
3
4
5
6
7
8
9
10
11
12
13
14
15

Exercise 4
Think of a few names for your brand that are way too general.

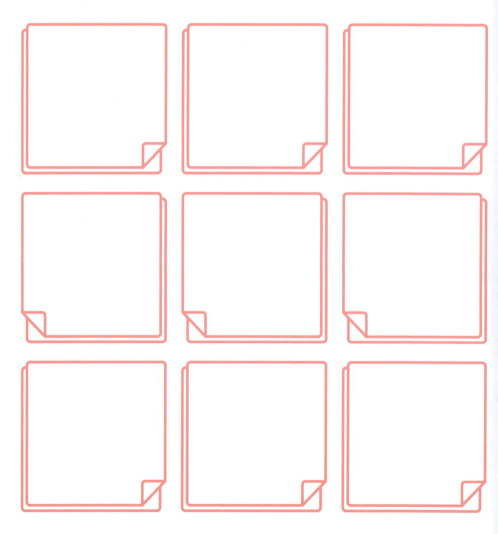

They don't mean anything: This is a fun one. Lots of people (particularly those who prioritize short URLs) like to name their companies after whatever short string of letters has an available dot com. I have no idea what a *Vongle* is. When naming, it's best to play off of connections that people already have in their heads. This way, when they hear your name, a picture will appear. When you pick a name that means absolutely nothing, it's hard to make the connection to what you're doing or how you feel about the world around you. It's easier to lump your brand in with all the other brands named after nothing—that is, if anyone can remember your random string of letters at all.

Exercise 5
Come up with a few names that don't mean anything. You know, things like *Blanderelk* and *ZZwhyG5* and *Utah Monday*.

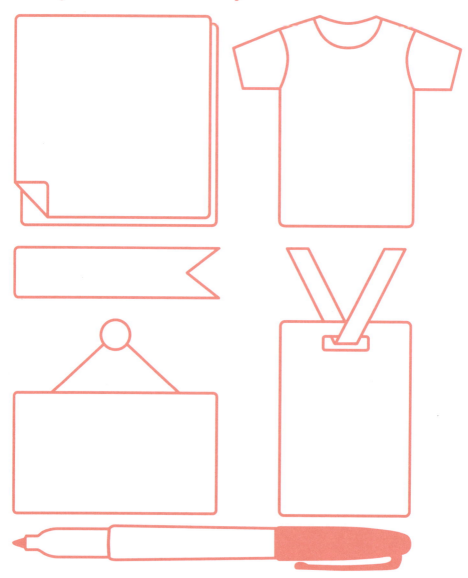

They're boring: See "names that are descriptive," "names that try and encompass everything."

They're on trend: Trends come and go. When the trend inevitably ends, your name will be frozen in time. Lots of cool restaurants these days have Blank & Blank names like *Bourbon & Beef, Fork & Vine, Salt & Time, Wolf & Hound.* When everyone moves onto the next trend, your name will start to look old. Great names should be timeless—not dying to fit in with a passing trend. How many people are dropping vowels like *Tumblr* and *Flickr* these days?

Exercise 6
Come up with a few names that are on trend.

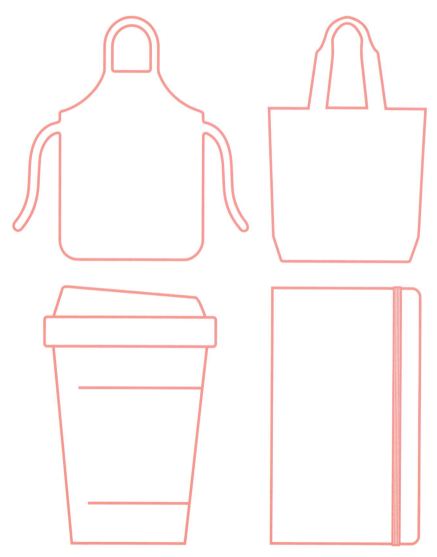

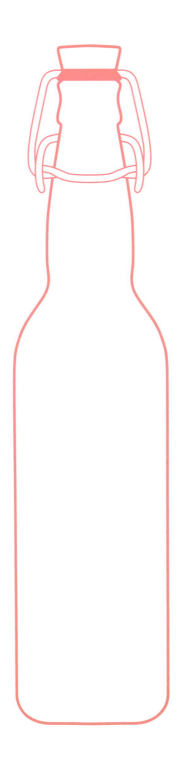

Kickshaw

Gus and Dave started a high-end wine delivery service in San Francisco. After working through *Don't Call It That* they settled on the name *Kickshaw*—a cool, archaic word meaning something small and elegant. Gus said *"Listing silly, inaccurate, and/or inappropriate names helped us focus on how we wanted our service to be perceived by customers. Ultimately, Don't Call It That helped us to hone a sharper and simpler vision of our concept."* Dave added *"We had some bad names, including 'Wine Dancer' (think Flashdance from the '80s), and 'Wine–1–1.' Everyone laughs when we say 'Wine–1–1.'"*

Ready, Set
The name is the start of the story.

The great names of the world have one
thing in common. They're about more than
selling people shit they don't need. They're
not just about trying to sway them with
marketing rhetoric. They're about speaking
the language of people in an effort to communicate something worth saying. They
have nerve, ambition, personality, a mission,
and, yes, they take risks. Because the easier
a name is to spell or pronounce or recognize
or understand or label, the easier it is to
forget. And there is nothing about a great
name that is forgettable. Your name is the
first word in your story about who you are
and why you matter—bad names get a story
off to a bad start. Think of your name as a
thesis statement: it's a way to inform and
curate the experience you're creating.

Making the simple complicated is commonplace; making the complicated simple, awesomely simple, that's creativity.

Charles Mingus

Get to the Point
Good names know what they're doing.

Naming becomes a lot easier when you have an objective—one thing you want the name to communicate. When you have an objective, it's easy to see past all the shallow criticism and find a name that gets the job done. The objective can really be anything, but a good place to start is: *What do I want my audience to feel when they hear my name?* Now, this isn't such an easy question. The answer needs to set you apart. The answer represents the kernel of your positioning.

Positioning is the art of showing people how you're different—what you do that your competitors don't. This difference can be physical (*Dyson* vacuums don't lose suction, *Freitag* bags are made of used truck tarpaulins) or it can take your mind somewhere unique (*Arc'teryx* evokes archaeology and dinosaurs instead of climbing Mount Everest).

Heads Up

"Positioning" is how you distinguish yourself from your closest competition. What's your advantage? How do you talk about what you do differently than they do? It could be a difference in product, audience, attitude, anything. This isn't a book on positioning, per se, but knowing how you want to set yourself apart from the competition can certainly set the stage for a great name.

For example, if you sell luxury watches you probably want to communicate that they're expertly crafted, precise, Swiss-made, that sort of thing. The problem is, all luxury watch companies say this. Now, you can join *Rolex* and *Omega* and *Patek Philippe* and try to beat them at their own game, but you're probably going to lose—they've been at this a long time and it's going to be hard to unseat them saying the same things they are. Besides, their marketing budgets are bigger than yours.

Thinking about names without first establishing your positioning is like selecting a box before buying the present that'll go in it. It's a decision without context.

Important:
Avoid trying to say you're the best, greatest, fastest, or most reliable at anything. It might be true, but people are so used to hearing it, they aren't going to believe you.

If they give you lined paper, write the other way.

William Carlos Williams

Heads Up

Start thinking of some feelings and ideas you want your name to communicate. How do you want to be different from your competition? How can you signal that with your name? Let's use the outdoor apparel company *Arc'teryx* as an example. A lot of outdoor apparel companies try to evoke the mountains: *The North Face, Mountain Hardware, Patagonia, Sierra Designs.* *Arc'teryx*, short for Archaeopteryx, makes you think of digging and paleontology. It's still about the outdoors, but decidedly different than its mountaineering predecessors.

Jumping Through Hoops
Naming without a checklist.

A lot of people like to put a bunch of requirements in place before they start coming up
with names. Not only does this make finding
a good name a needle-in-a-haystack exercise,
but most of these requirements aren't well
founded. Let's look at a few of the most
common barriers that people erect to make
naming more complicated than it has to be:

URL:
Look, we all know it's hard to find a
straightaway dot com. This means that
most people who spend any time on the
internet are pretty tolerant and forgiving
when it comes to URLs. That said, not
everyone needs a URL as pure as the driven
snow. While clearly the first choice is to
have yourbrandname.com, its unavailability
should almost never be a deal breaker.
A lot of people get caught looking for a URL
instead of a name. Don't join their ranks.

First you need to think about how your core audiences will end up at your website. Will you speak with them first? Will they see you in an online banner ad? Will they search for you on *Google*? In most of these cases, they won't be directly typing your URL into the browser—they'll have some help. A study by Forrester, a leading business and technology advisory group, finds that 93 percent of online experiences begin with a search. So even if your business exists entirely online, most people will be getting to your site through search engines and other links. Modern browsers like Chrome and Safari include search in the address bar making it even easier to find where you're trying to go.

Heads Up

If people want to find you, chances are they will (even if you're a startup). You probably shouldn't be focusing too much attention on the sort of consumer who gives up on finding you after yourbrandname.com doesn't take them to the right place.

If your entire business doesn't exist exclusively on the internet, you're probably better off finding a strong name that grabs people's attention and then finding a URL that works. Most people understand the reality of getting a URL these days and won't hold it against you if you don't have a pure dot com. If you're confident in what you're doing and how you're doing it, having a slightly modified URL will not be a big obstacle for you.

There are thousands of very successful businesses that use dot net or some other creative URL extension. As long as the dot com isn't a big or related business, another domain extension is a viable option. Some people think that if you don't have a dot com, customers will think you don't have a serious business. To them I say that a URL isn't the only way to show people you have a serious business. Having a well-designed site certainly helps, and so does a little publicity. Some very successful sites that didn't worry about having a dot com include americanapparel.net, last.fm, angel.co, rapha.cc, good.is, canopy.co, and *Google's* parent company *Alphabet* (abc.xyz). Again, if people are using a search engine to find you, having a dot net isn't a big deal. In the case of *Good*, they used the country extension for Iceland in their URL. In most cases you don't have to do business in a country in order to use their extensions and you can create some pretty interesting options that are probably available. Other potentially useful extensions are: .as, .at, .be, .by, .co, .ee, .in, .it, .ly, and .to. You can view all of them here: ahundredmonkeys.com/dcit.

In the end, URLs are a losing battle. The number of available dot coms that are even remotely pronounceable in English is small and declining rapidly. Hell, Elon Musk didn't even get his hands on tesla.com until 2016—well after he established a thriving empire. According to research by WhoAPI, zero four-letter URLs are available to be registered, so I hope you didn't have your heart set on qbmz.com. On the other hand, the general population is becoming more and more web-savvy. At some point in the not-too-distant future, dot coms are going to be an anachronism. Don't let this be the thing that gets between you and coming up with the right name for your business.

Pronounceability and spell-ability:
A lot of people want names that are edgy, imaginative, and inimitable, but only so long as they're also easy to spell, easy to say, and impossible to forget. The only trouble being, easy and evocative are natural enemies. Nothing is so sure to slip

between the ears undetected as the word that requires no effort to absorb.

We remember best that which asks something of us. So, embrace the difficult, the strange, the bizarre. And if you want people to remember you, embrace the one thing that will help them do just that: stand out. There's no point in coming up with a name that makes you sound like everyone else and then spending a bunch of money on marketing that tries to convince them you're different. A good name can do the work for you, but only if you let it.

At the heart of anything good there should be a kernel of something undefinable, and if you can define it, or claim to be able to define it, then, in a sense, you've missed the point.

John Peel

One thing that strong names have in common is the ease with which they can be attacked and dismissed. For example, imagine that you were in the corporate meetings where the following names were put on the table. After each name are possible comments, any of which would be sufficient to kiss that name goodbye:

Apple
- Full of worms
- Easily bruised
- Fall from grace
- Doesn't sound like a computer
- What kind of education are we talking about here?

Virgin Atlantic
- Says "We're new at this"
- Nobody will take us seriously
- Unprofessional
- Religious people will be offended

Banana Republic
- Ugly racial stereotype
- You'll be picketed by people from small, hot countries
- Do you import produce?

So given all of this surface negativity, why do these names work? What would you have needed to know in order to have predicted their success, rather than their failure? A name acquires the personality traits you give it. Branding and design are used to help people see a name in the light you're intending.

Kids These Days
Josh Shipp is a former at-risk foster kid turned teen advocate. He's a best-selling author and has been featured on *Good Morning America, Oprah*, MTV, CNN and *The New York Times*. Josh used *Don't Call It That* to name his organization. *Kids These Days* creates school curriculum, products, and live events for parents, teachers, and

caring adults. The curriculum is being used in 2,100 schools worldwide. The goal is to teach kids real life skills in a genuine and engaging way—all the stuff you should have learned in school but probably didn't.

"If you're going to have the nerve to open your mouth, publish something, speak on something... what's the point of doing that timidly?"

Kids These Days doesn't shy away from negativity. It actually aligns itself with it. *"The name is clear. People are familiar with it. It's typically a negative thing. 'Get off my lawn, get off your iPhone!' The name starts with something people are saying anyway. It isn't overly optimistic. When you own the baggage it shows that you get it, that you understand the problem. Yes, kids are frustrating. But they're amazing at the same time. In order for us to get to the solution, it was stronger for us to align with the problem and show that we get it."*

Remember, interesting names have a back-story—they come from somewhere, they arouse curiosity. And no story worth your time is all sunshine, smiles, and rainbows. Every name has weaknesses. Every word that isn't clichéd to death isn't a flawless representation of beauty, strength, and speed. This is what it means to be human— embrace it. Don't fall into the same Valium-induced stupor where you'll find words like "synergy," "innovation," and "solutions"— words acting like not-so-radiant beacons, telling the world you want to be just like everyone else.

I'm at war obvious.

William Eggleston

with the

Make Some Headroom
Naming in the right frame of mind.

First things first, you're going to need to
get comfortable. Being creative comes easy
to some people and is a lot harder for
others. Creativity is not innate. It's a skill
that takes practice to develop. So for start-
ers, get out of your normal work environment. Get away from the distractions, the
emails, the TPS reports. Find somewhere
(with internet access) that feels like a
comfortable thinking space without any
distractions. Now have a beer or three and
it's time to get naming.

Exercise 7

Let's come up with some good names for a new streaming music service.

There are no rules when coming up with names—just come up with cool shit. There is no why, no how, in this phase. No checking URLs or asking other people. Just write everything down that comes to mind.

Heads Up

It is helpful to work on something you aren't so emotionally tied to at first. It's similar to how people have a much easier time telling their friends how to handle their relationships than they have figuring out their own.

Come up with some names here:

1
2
3
4
5
6
7
8
9
10
11
12
13
14
15

Now let's quickly shift into coming up with good names for your project. Anything goes, as long as "anything" isn't snore-inducing. Think of some risky names, some names your mom would get mad at you for, some names that will make people ask *"What does that mean?"*.

Here are some questions that might help you along:

What feeling do you want to evoke in your audience?

What are the main actions you're trying to get people to do?

If your company were a rare plant or animal, which would it be?

What analogies can you come up with for how your business operates?

How would you explain your project to a five-year-old in a way that would keep him or her interested?

Does the concept of what you're trying to accomplish exist in other industries? Do they use different words to describe this concept?

What are a few good metaphors for what you're doing?

What role in people's lives are you aspiring to fill?

It might be hard for you to think beyond the literal answers to these questions. To this I say, you're going to need to come up with non-literal answers to these questions whether you're naming or not.

Come up with some names here:

1 _____

2 _____

3 _____

4 _____

5 _____

6 _____

7 _____

8 _____

9 _____

10 _____

11 _____

12 _____

13 _____

14 _____

15 _____

_____

_____

_____

_____

_____

Ch. 6

People don't want to be sold a product or a service, they want to be sold an idea. They want to understand how their lives are going to be better with your company in it. The literal, along with basic concepts like *"it's faster,"* and *"it's more reliable,"* doesn't cut it. Sure, they might be integral to what you're doing, but you need to look past your customers as workers or employees. They're people, and people don't always make calculated logical decisions. They want to be excited and intrigued.

Exercise 8
What idea are you selling?

The Attention Deficit

First job of naming: getting people to give a shit.

One of the biggest mistakes people make in branding is drastically overestimating the degree to which people care about what you're doing. This leads companies to want to explain their whole offering before even checking to see if the audience is interested. It's like going on a first date and telling your whole life story—probably not going to work out so well. Generating interest isn't typically about throwing a ton of information out there.

In baiting a mousetrap with cheese, always leave room for the mouse.

Saki

You need to show people how you make their lives better. You need to get them to a place where they're interested in learning more on their own. Arouse their curiosity. To get there, you're going to need a name that draws them in.

What draws people in?
- mystery
- obscurity
- romance
- subtlety
- comedy
- confidence

Don't think about these words specifically, but think about how you can use other words, in combination with what you're doing, to create these feelings for people.

Examples:

Cruel World
A job hunting site

Inkling
An iPad-based learning company

Retrofit
High-tech weight loss for business professionals

Riverbed
A large-scale data transfer company

Mechanical Turk
On-demand, scalable workforce

Teenage Engineering
Electronic music controllers

Arrogant Bastard
Strong beer

Band of Outsiders
Fashion label

See how none of these names are trying to explain anything? Even better, they aren't trying to sell you at all. Instead of being a sales pitch, these names work to establish a feeling. They're interesting and memorable on their own. Try forgetting a beer called *Arrogant Bastard*. Good luck.

Show Don't Tell
Why "trust me" says "don't trust me."

Running a naming company, you come across a lot of *Brand Attributes*. Hell, we even create our fair share of them. It seems like everyone wants their brand to be trust- worthy, approachable, fun, engaging, and innovative. Aside from being borderline meaningless clichés, it would be great to have a brand that was actually all of these things. The problem is, trust and innova- tion need to be earned. Saying you're inno- vative, or that you value innovation, buys you nothing. The only way to be perceived as being innovative is to actually do innova- tive things. The only way to be trustworthy is to build a rapport with someone, earn their trust, and respect it once you have it.

Interestingly, there's actually an inverse effect at play here. When someone says they're trustworthy, your inclination is not to trust them. Using the word "trustworthy" feels untrustworthy. Another example comes to mind. There's a hole in the wall pizzeria on Gough Street in San Francisco with a sign that says "World famous pizza!" We both know there is nothing world famous about their pizza. If there was a world famous pizzeria nearby, you'd know about it—there'd be a line out the door. Saying you're world famous does little more than show that you're not.

So when we have a company come to us and say it's paramount that their name conveys trust, we need to find another way in. While trust needs to be built and earned, what makes someone seem trustworthy? While a lot of things from posture to eye contact play into it, confidence and honesty make us inclined to trust someone. The confident person doesn't say "trust me," they make you feel safe. Airlines are a good industry to look at as an example. The most important thing for airlines is safety. When you get on a plane, you're trusting that airline with your life while you hurtle through the sky in a metal tube at five hundred miles per hour. How many big airlines have "trust" or "safety" in their name? None. This is because they know that using these words actually has the opposite effect. *Virgin Airways* is a great example. Their name, taken at face value, says that they're new to flying. If you were literal-minded in trying to convey safety and security, this name would look like a terrifying proposition. What the name *Virgin* does have is tons of confidence. And confidence is exactly what you're looking for in an airline you're trusting with your life.

So if you're trying to use brand attributes as a foundation for coming up with names, it's important to ask yourself how you convey the feeling of your brand attributes. It's almost never a good idea to actually use the words or their synonyms in naming.

Wordsmash
Lexical synergy or a head-on collision?

There's a big naming misconception in corporate America. It would appear that a lot of companies have gotten the idea that if you smash two words together, people are somehow going to place you at the mental intersection of these two word's definitions. *Comcast* casts communications. *Instagram* lets you make records instantly. *Verizon* is apparently what happens when you see truth (veritas) on the horizon.

At *A Hundred Monkeys* we call this Word-smash. So while these companies have massive advertising budgets to drive recognition of these lexical collisions, they in no way place themselves at the nexus of these concepts. No matter how much you believe in subliminal messaging, when you hear *Verizon* you are not going to think "Oh, veritas horizon!" Even if you did... what would it buy them?

If you're just starting out and don't have the money to jam a new word into people's heads, picking a name that grabs attention and connects to what you're doing in an interesting way is a much better approach.

TURNCOAT

Lusk

IZOLA

HYALINE

LONGROY

STRAYS attic

VOLTAGE salt

BANLIEU

Kids, Dogs, Goldfish
What you aren't naming.

Naming a company or product isn't like naming anything else. There is an entirely different set of parameters. This is interesting because a lot of people name companies like they're naming their kids. Having a name like *Data Aggregation Solutions* or *Thrivent* is like naming your kid *John* or *Sarah*. Nothing stands out. Only problem is, in this game you don't want to be the kid no one remembers. You want to be the one they can't forget. And you can't accomplish that with a name that says you're afraid to stand out. So who cares if someone makes fun of your name every once in awhile? If you have some confidence in what you're doing it's a non-issue.

There's risk built into standing out.

I think we all intuitively know this. Any time you tell a joke or a funny story, there's a chance people won't laugh—and that's embarrassing. What people don't talk about, though, is the risk you take when you don't stand out. Naming, branding, positioning, marketing are all about engage-ment—getting people's attention to the point where they actually send something back your way. There is absolutely nothing engaging about a name that makes you sound like everyone else. So you tell your-self you're going to stand out some other way. Are you?

And even if you are, if your audience balks at your name, there's a pretty big chance you're not going to get that opportunity anyway. So when you actually think about it, not having an engaging name represents a pretty big risk.

MadSam Studios

Jason Smithers used *Don't Call It That* during a studio rebrand. *"We started with* Itsthemix.com, *but it was so generic and* every audio mixing studio offering online services has 'mix' in the title. After working through the book, we settled on MadSam Studios."

The name came from the engineer's two children, Sam and Madison. "When people ask about the name, it opens us up to talk about us being family guys. We only do the studio thing because it's our passion. We aren't out to make a ton of money and waste time we could be spending with family. Itsthemix was just confusing for people and really had no meat. Our thinking was originally when people ask about what the name means we'd say something like 'Your mix makes or breaks your song. It's all about the mix' but that's usually where the conversation ended. We have found we've created deeper relationships with our clients because we're personable and just your average guys raising families and making music."

Exercise 9
What are some names for your brand that people will never forget?

I'm with Stupid
Don't do naming for idiots.

Companies these days don't seem to think much of their customers. This is readily apparent when you look at naming. People are afraid to use names that are hard to spell or aren't immediately understandable to someone with a third grade education. They think that if people can't spell it, there's no way they're going to want to associate with it. This is a bad mistake for a few reasons:

1/ *Everyone does it:*
With everyone playing to the lowest common denominator, a very easy way to separate yourself is to establish a brand that isn't so remedial.

2/ *People spend more time on something they don't understand right away:*
Since we run into a few hundred names a day (at least), we need a reason to pay attention. Not understanding something

right away is a great reason for someone to pay attention. Hell, they might even look it up.

3/ *Everything isn't for everyone:*
One of the biggest reasons people try to appeal to the lowest common denominator is that they want their company to appeal to everyone. Hate to break it to you (them), but nothing is for everyone. Sex and chocolate aren't even for everyone. In fact, you run a bigger risk turning off the one or two audiences who are really important to you by trying to appeal to anyone with a pulse. People are attracted to brands that speak to them. It's hard to have a real conversation with someone when you're worried about what everyone else is going to think. Focus on your customer. If you're successful at communicating with them, they'll pitch other people for you.

4/ *People like to play up a level:*
Remember when you were in middle school and you thought high schoolers were so cool and grown up? They can drive! Remember when you were in high school and you thought you really belonged in college? We want what we don't have. This applies to love, money, and even knowledge. So just because people might not understand your name or brand right away, doesn't mean they aren't going to be attracted to it. Sometimes aiming over people's heads is a great way to get their attention. What percentage of people who walk into a *Starbucks* know where the name comes from? (*Moby Dick.*)

5/ *If the people you're trying to communicate with are college educated, don't pretend they aren't:*
People like it when you appeal to their intelligence. They like to associate with "smart" brands. And if they don't understand your name or how to spell it, that's what *Google* is for.

Figure out who your most important audience is. Find out how to grab their attention. Don't worry about appeasing them yet— that's not a job for a name. Just try to get a reaction: a smile, a question, a genuine laugh, even an inquisitive glance.

Exercise 10
Who is your most important audience?

1
2
3
4
5
6
7
8
9
10

Who is your most important audience? Circle one from each column.

Rugged	Imaginary	Luddites
Fiery	Lost	Hippies
Blithe	Taciturn	Millennials
Belligerent	Traveling	Tesla drivers
Skeptical	Exacting	1%ers
Boisterous	Reactionary	Dual citizens
Canny	Evangelical	Athletes
Adventurous	Progressive	Coders
Mysterious	Mustachioed	Long-haul truckers
Absurdist	Lewd	Academics
Calculating	Romantic	Parents
Protective	Laconic	Artists
Hopeful	Carnivorous	Engineers
Righteous	Voyeuristic	Alcoholics
Persistent	Practical	Gonzo journalists
Theatrical	Articulate	Dreamers
Domineering	Verbose	Amateur chefs
Salty	Experienced	Ex-pats
Over-eager	Predictable	Teens
Myopic	Laid-back	Medical pros

Don't Reinvent the Wheel
Where do good names come from?

Some names are created and others are found. *Spotify*, *Snapchat*, and *WhatsApp* were created. *Apple*, *Virgin*, *Nike*, and *Starbucks* were found—that is to say, these words existed before big brands starting using them. Of course, there's plenty of gray area, too. Names like *Snapchat* and *Evernote* simply combine two words that we all know. Names like *Flickr*, *Tumblr*, and *Waze* are derivatives and misspellings of common words.

When it comes to developing names on your own, you should almost always be in the mode of finding words. Maybe issues like URL scarcity and trademark availability force you to drop vowels or smash words together in a pinch, but this should never be your approach to coming up with names. There are so many great words that are not commonly used—words you can own and define for your audience. Made-up words usually take a lot of work for people to remember and don't have any cool associations built in. Sure, they're ownable, but it's a bit like buying a tiny plot of land in the middle of the desert and trying to turn it into a tourist attraction. So for now, it's best to think of yourself as an explorer on the lookout for cool words and phrases that you can relate to your brand in an interesting way.

IMBROGLIO

NO

PICNIC

STRAYS VOLTAGE

IZOLA

WIRE
FOX

Young
Villains

* *

HYPERNYM

While some of these words are easy to find. Others are hidden in dictionaries of regional English and old magazines. Easy-to-find names are usually hard to acquire and own because they're so frequently used. This is why it's a good idea to look off the beaten path.

EthosWell

Sarah Merion is the Founder and CEO of *EthosWell*, a site that connects people with complementary healthcare providers such as chiropractors, acupuncturists, and dietitians. Originally she had been trying to invent names. *"I was complicating things. It's easy to over think when you're coming up with names. The book helped simplify the creative process and bound the scope of what I was trying to do. Knowing that I didn't need to make up words was really helpful for me. Instead I was able to use words in interesting, new ways. You don't have to be an inventor. If the associations aren't there with your invented words, they don't do you much good."*

Heads Up

Two particularly fruitful areas to find names: Proper nouns (people, places, things) from stories, myths, music, history: Atticus, Xanadu, Tecumseh, Crystal Ship, Clangor.

Obscure words from trades, science, culture: Syzygy, Wingbox, Status Symbol, Warbler, Cresset.

The Power of Isolation
Some words are better on their own.

Names can assume a different character when you abstract them from the sentences and paragraphs in which we're accustomed to seeing them. A lot of popular names like *Square, Apple,* and *Gap* feel pedestrian when you look at their traditional usage and definitions. When you isolate them they feel more powerful and ubiquitous. It's like taking an unknown actor and giving them a leading role. Elevating them, betting on them, makes others take a longer look and try to see what you're seeing.

While we are talking about isolating words, the context in which the names will be seen is still very important. *Apple* would never work as a fruit company. From a legal standpoint, it would be unprotectable because you cannot prevent people from describing their goods. Finding these simple words in contexts where you wouldn't expect them does two things. It makes people curious because they aren't used to seeing a name in this light. It also happens to be much more protectable from a legal standpoint.

Palace is unexpected for a skate company. For that matter, so is *Girl. Mother* as a name for an ad agency makes you stop and think. Elevating these words to leading roles in unfamiliar contexts makes for interesting names.

Exercise 11
Come up with some words that feel fresh on their own.

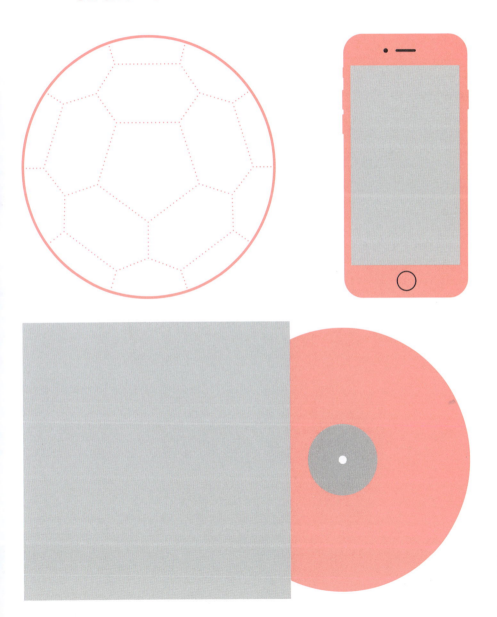

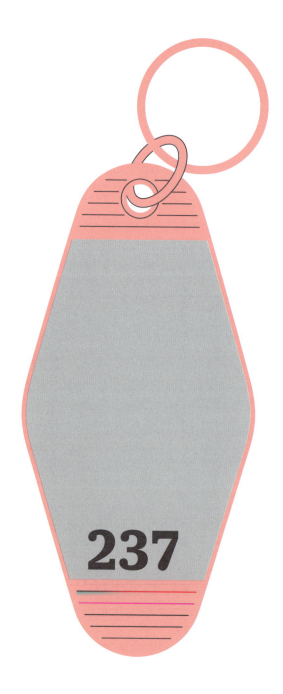

New Species Discovered Daily
Name taxonomy.

So let's come up with some more names. This time let's be sure we're getting into new territory. We're going to do this by looking at a taxonomy of sorts. Let's look at the different types of names that are out in the wild.

Before *PETA* had so much influence, the expression was, *"There's more than one way to skin a cat."* If you're trying to name a company or a product, there are, in fact, a lot of ways to go.

The general consensus (especially amongst lawyers) seems to be that there are two types of names: *descriptive* and *evocative*. It's a bit like saying there are two kinds of food: savory and sweet. (Where do you put kettle corn?!) It's somewhat true in a clinically technical capacity, but when you're coming up with names, thinking of the world in terms of these two categories is dry and unhelpful.

Yes, descriptive and evocative are two big phyla, but I'd like to dive in a little and look at all the species. So far at *A Hundred Monkeys* we have come up with 29 different types of names and we're still looking. This is not an analysis. We're not talking pros and cons. If you're trying to name a company or a product, there are, in fact, more options than you think.

Types of company/product names:

Poetic
Names that paint a picture or roll off the tongue

Bumble and bumble / AIAIAI / Lululemon

High Class Gibberish
Where do they come from? An ancient dictionary? Outer space?

Kodak / Zynga / Xerox

Derivative
Almost something you've heard of

Nespresso / Arc'teryx / Zappos

Initials
The easy way out

KFC / BMW / ESPN

Acronyms
Initials that you say instead of spell

Asics / SAAB / RAND

Interesting Letters
Letters that go above and beyond

TCHO / RAV4 / THX

Descriptive
Just get to the point

Airbus / VitaminWater / Whole Foods

Part Descriptive, Part Fun
You might as well have some fun along the way

Juicy Couture / Mighty Leaf / Big Gulp

Part Descriptive, Part Emotional
We've got soul™

Zendesk / SoulCycle / Zenefits

Americana
Names that awaken feelings of patriotism

Baby Ruth / Dixon Ticonderoga / 76 gasoline

Into the Wild
Nature as powerful inspiration

Patagonia / Juniper Ridge / Wolf Ranges

Someone Special

The man, the myth, the legend

Tesla Motors / Jack Daniel's / Newman's Own

Made-up People

Pure invention with a dose of reality

Warby Parker / Dr. Pepper / Captain Morgan

Remember When

Names that feel like they've been around for a while

Banana Republic / Old Milwaukee / Crown Royal

Suggests the Solution

What's in it for me?

Kryptonite / SubZero / 5-hour Energy

Back to Basics

Everything else is so complicated

Free People / Simple shoes / Country Time

Daring

Not for the faint of heart

Obey / Virgin / Big Ass Fans

Adrenaline
Get your motor running

Stingray / Speedo / Full Throttle

Foreign-feeling
Implied sophistication

Clinique / Häagen-Dazs / Tazo

Literary/Historical
Align yourself with something powerful

Starbucks / Big Bertha / Rosetta Stone

Place Names
Names that take you somewhere

Lonely Planet / Hidden Valley Ranch / Oaklandish

One Letter Off
So close yet so far

Shyp / Zillow / Lyft

Vowel Dropper's Anonymous
Auto-correct's worst nightmare

Flickr / Tumblr / Unbxd

Mythical
A lot to live up to

Nike / Pandora / Hermès

Exclamation
Something to get excited about

I Can't Believe It's Not Butter! / Yelp! / Buzz Off!

Name as Statement
Names that are on a mission

Forever 21 / True Religion / LiveStrong

Latin Class
Veni, vidi, vici

ExOfficio / Novartis / Prorsum

Utilitarian
Names your grandpa would be proud of

Madewell / Cut-Rite / Bi-Rite

Blank & Blank
These are things you remind me of

Crate & Barrel / Bourbon & Branch / Bot & Dolly

While there are so many different routes to finding a great name, everyone seems to pick from the same two or three groups. Think about why the names from the expanded list of categories work—and how they help their companies get people's attention and start to tell a story. Expand your horizons a bit—it's good for you. Come up with some new names in these new categories. What would be the most risqué name you could pick? What's the best mythical name you can come up with? This search takes equal servings of creativity and research. Don't be afraid to look under some rocks. Get lost in *Wikipedia* looking at extinct sea creatures. Explore some fictional characters from the 1800s. With naming, getting lost is one of the best ways to end up with a name that will get you found. Just be on the lookout for an interesting thread—a cool way to tie potential names to what you're doing. Trust me, everyone has already found the boring ways.

*I want to feel like a gold miner, and
I don't want the gold given to me.*

John Baldessari

Push and Pull
Same name, different meaning.

While words have their own qualities and associations, context is the lens through which names are viewed in the real world. The same word can transform dramatically in the contexts of different businesses and industries. Let's look at how a few names (some real, some fictional) are perceived in different situations:

ACE
Ace Hardware
Ace Hotel
Ace Ammunition

STANDARD
Standard Accounting
Standard Caviar
Standard Cement

Standard Accounting feels boring. Saying "normal" in accounting is not helpful. It reinforces negative stereotypes of accountants being boring and by-the-book.

Standard Caviar is interesting. There's some contrast between the luxury of caviar and the established level of standard. In this context "Standard" feels modern, almost brash.

Standard Cement, while not being too vibrant or differentiated, has an industrial feel to it that probably has some appeal your average construction worker or contractor.

Words that feel expected in one industry can play with the perception, tropes, or ideals of another. How a word like "standard" comes to life in certain situations while being rendered inert in other contexts is part of the appeal.

16

Apples and Alligators
Names aren't brands, yet.

Remember: any name that's already in use isn't just a name. It's supported by a logo and a website and a myriad of other things that bring it to life. If everything works according to plan, a name and a brand end up meaning the same thing in people's minds. But that's not the case when you start out. At the beginning, a name is just a word or two on a sheet of paper next to a bunch of other words and maybe a doodle of Bart Simpson.

Seeing the potential isn't always easy. So when you're comparing your names against the competition, remember that you're comparing a nascent name with an existing brand. It's a little like looking at a baby and saying, *"There's no way he'll be the next Steph Curry."* Not with that attitude he won't.

Instead, focus on your objective. What is the name supposed to communicate to my audience? Does this name sound different from my competitors' names? Is this name going to be a good vessel for holding my story and products and experiences? If you can focus on these things, your name will have everything it needs to develop into a thriving brand. Remember, the name is just the beginning of your story—don't put more weight on it than you have to.

Staging names in the environments that your audience would normally come in contact with your brand is also helpful. So if you're building a website, you could try mocking up your homepage. If you're starting a restaurant, you could make a sample menu. Evaluating names in a realistic environment is a lot more valuable than looking at them on a blank page.

Exercise 12
What are your competitors' names?

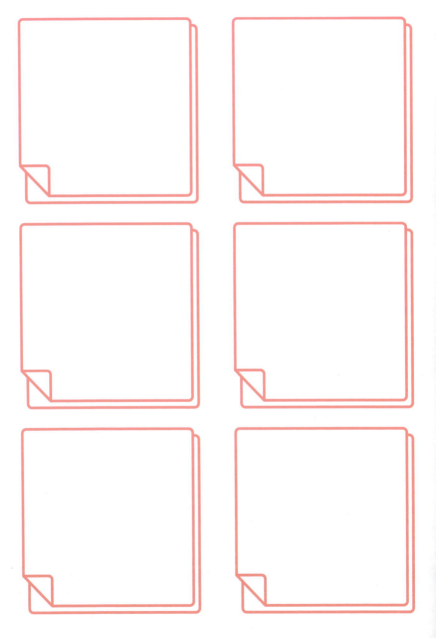

Exercise 13
What are some names that would stand out next to your competitors? Try them out in context.

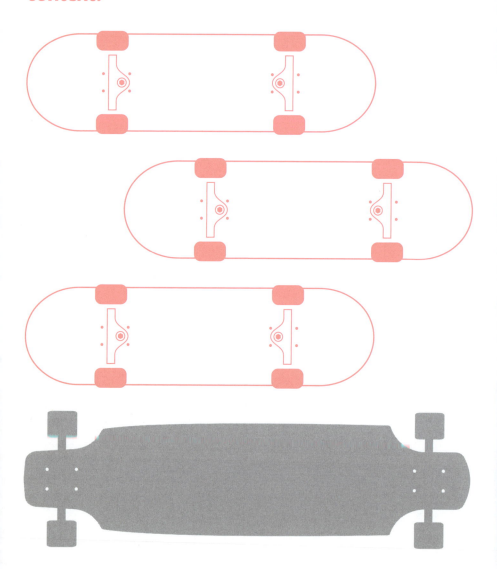

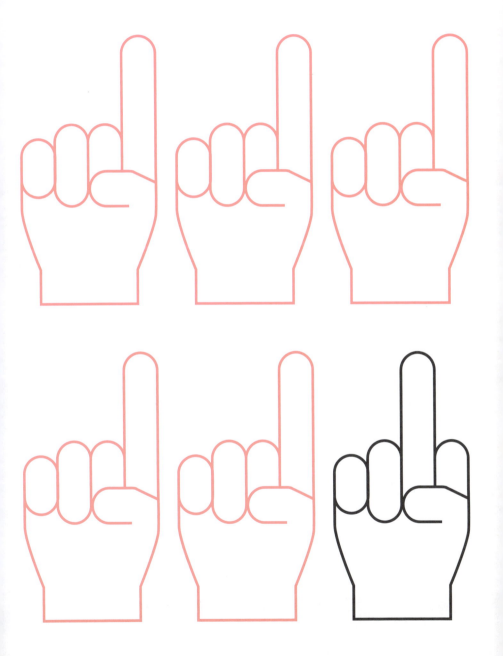

Love at First Sight
Why naming isn't a romantic comedy.

Something I hear a lot is that people will know the right name when they hear it. They want to be blown away by a name. They want to fall in love instantly. This couldn't be farther from reality. It's a little like seeing a girl/guy in a bar and knowing you're going to marry them before you start talking. It's romantic, and life would be a lot easier if this happened to people, but it's not how the world works. Names, like relationships, can be a perfect fit—they just never start out that way. You have to grow into them. If you're looking for perfection from the start you're going to go home empty-handed.

Even if you do somehow fall in love with a name, what's the likelihood it's available? So let's save the storybook romance for Disney movies and take more of a practical approach with naming.

Names Are Living Beings
Perception is reality.

Arriving at a name is really just the beginning. Names are living vessels that collect all of the interactions, experience and news for your brand. Everything new you do gets tied back to your name. While this makes assessing new names difficult, it's what gives lasting brands their brand equity and reputation. Releasing a product or launching a new advertising campaign affects what your name means to people. Some of these effects are within your control while others are not. In 2014, *ISIS Chocolate of Belgium* saw a sharp decline in sales. Did it have anything to do with their chocolate? No. *Wikipedia* cites 11 companies and organizations that have changed names due to the rise of ISIS in Iraq and Syria. This list also includes the mobile payment venture of *AT&T, T-Mobile,* and *Verizon.* Even with their combined marketing clout, they wanted no part of ISIS.

What once brought to mind an Egyptian goddess now evokes violent extremism.

So while it's a natural feeling to want to control every aspect of how a name and brand is perceived, it's important to accept that some of it will always be outside of your control. The more popular you become, the more likely it is that parts of your brand will grow beyond your control. Look at how many times *Nike* and *Facebook* and *Chanel* get misappropriated. People print Swooshes on acid tabs! While most of these giants vigorously defend their marks, it just means that they've grown so large within our collective consciousness they've become part of the zeitgeist.

19

How to Ask Friends
Don't.

If you ask people what they think, you're sure to end up with more opinions than you can safely manage. It is best to keep it between yourself and the few people you trusted enough to start this crazy project to begin with. That means not inviting every developer, former colleague, and old friend to join the conversation—even if they say they "have marketing experience" or "have named a few things before."

Nothing ruins creativity like too many voices weighing in. We call it the *Ice Cream Principle.* Tell 10 people to go get ice cream with one condition: they all have to agree on one flavor. That flavor is going to be chocolate or vanilla every time. Groups of people don't agree on what's cool or interesting, they agree on what's easy to agree on. Don't pick a name strictly because it's the top vote-getter.

This applies to focus groups, too. A lot of people try to focus group or "A/B test" names. It is seen as "safe" because you're letting consumers make decisions for you. This is not what focus groups are for. They're for learning about people's problems and desires and understanding where they are coming from. Focus groups are not supposed to make decisions for you. So while there are a lot of good reasons to do focus groups, naming is not one of them.

As Dan Pallotta points out in his *Harvard Business Review* blog post "Real Leaders Don't Do Focus Groups" [ahundredmonkeys. com/dcit], asking someone what they think when it comes to something creative is a pretty clear signal that you're lacking confidence.

This applies to naming. You can't focus group names because creativity is hard to test and harder to quantify. It would be like using scientific analysis to find great art.

It doesn't work that way. The environment of the focus group is entirely contrived.

People are never asked about how they feel about names devoid of context. They're used to seeing names as part of a bigger whole— live companies and products in the real world. Attempting to isolate the name as a variable is unnatural and foreign to the people you would be asking. This, however, does not mean these people won't be happy to give you their opinion, typically delivered in a manner disproportionately forceful relative to how they actually feel about it.

Heads Up

If you're ever going to involve other people, you need to do it in a way that simulates the way they would actually come in contact with a name in the real world. "I was thinking about maybe naming my company *Orbiter*, what do you think?" is not a question people are equipped to answer.

Exercise 14
What are your favorite names you've come up with so far?

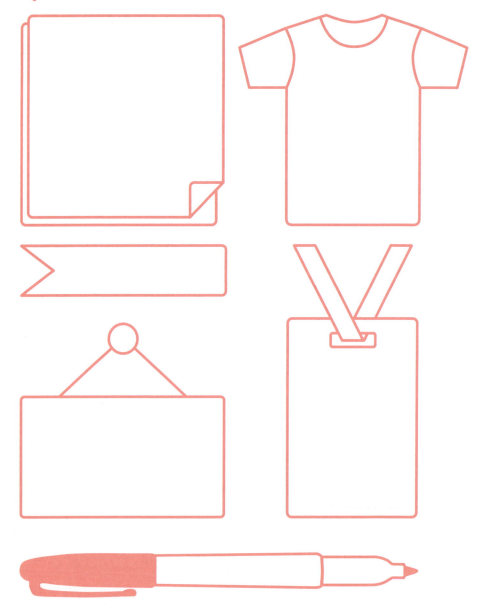

20

Climbing Over Clichés

Your business is bigger than a web address.

There are a lot of garden variety names that have been clichéd to death. For a while in the '90s everyone seemed to be into Latin words—so academic and classical. After that came vowel-dropping: *Flickr, Tumblr, Dopplr*. These names exist primarily because of URL scarcity. Can't get pasture. com? Try *Pastur*! Engine.com taken? No worries, try *Engin*!

The problem here is that you're looking for a name for your company, not just a URL. Repeat after me:

"My name is bigger than my URL." Say it a few times. A lot of people over-prioritize their URL because they think their company only exists on the web. Problem is, every company, no matter how web-centric, also exists in real life (or IRL for you alternate-reality types). We all spend a lot of time

telling people what we do. We hand out business cards and talk to potential partners. Your name is just as important here as it is on the web. And when people ask you why you're called *Engin*, *"...because engine-with-an-e wasn't available"* is not a good answer. Neither is, *"Whatever, it's just something we came up with. It works for now."* Answers like these do not help your case.

Talent Show

Abe Vizcarra used *Don't Call It That* to help him name his collaborative design studio in Los Angeles. Abe said *"I wanted something that was a bit utilitarian. Talent Show is common vernacular so people are familiar with it, but not in this context. It's not meant to be taken literally. I was looking to get a reaction. The name is about showcasing not only our own talent, but the talent of our partners and clients, too. It's always a collaboration."* But it wasn't a eureka moment (it rarely is). *"When I first came up with the name I was curious and skeptical. Then the doubt started to settle in. Can I get a URL? I started having my doubts. Really though, you can poke holes in anything. But it's like a new pair of jeans. The fit is a little rough at first, but as you wear them, they really start to shape around you and the way you move."*

To Verb or Not to Verb
Can a "verbable" name help you?

One of the most common things clients ask for in a name is the ability to use it as a verb.
"Google it."
"Skype me."
"Photoshop that."
"Let's Lyft there."

While some names lend themselves to "verbing" better than others, it's really more a factor of popularity than the ease with which a name can be used as a verb. Looking at the examples above, when people were first introduced to *Google* and *Skype*, the names lacked associations. This makes it easy to interpret an unknown word as a noun or a verb. *Photoshop* is a clunky name. It does contain two words that can both be used as nouns and verbs but "Photoshop it" has a lot more to do with it being an industry standard than any sort of implicit "verbability."

"Just Twitter it" doesn't have a ring to it, but *"tweet it"* does. Either way, without critical mass getting adoption for an invented verb is a fool's errand. If your name has poetry or is fun to say, and is relatively short, you're putting yourself in "verbable" territory. Now you just need a few million fans.

Exercise 15
Take your verbs for a spin.

	it.

	me.

	that.

Let's ☐ there.

I ☐ therefore I am.

	it.

	me.

	that.

Let's ☐ there.

I ☐ therefore I am.

Field Exercise
What your name says about you.

Let's look at an interaction we've all had a bunch of times.

So far you've confirmed your worst nightmares about CloudX'16. Nothing about a "Mid-Market Cloud Expo" sounded like a good idea. Yet, there you are in your $200 jeans and factory-faded polo. Your continental breakfast is lodged somewhere behind your sternum and is working its way down, or up...hard to tell.

"Hi, I'm Sarah."
"Oh, hello there."
"What do you do?"
"I'm the CMO for *Omnitau*, we make cloud apps."
"Oh, cool," says Sarah, maintaining an almost uncomfortable level of eye contact. You return the favor.
"So what do you do Sarah?"

"I work for Klipspringer."
"What's *Klipspringer*?"
"It's a relative of the antelope that lives in the African grasslands. It can jump 15 times its height to see predators above the tall grass."
"Ha, cool."
"Yeah, we do cloud analytics. It's easy to get caught in the weeds. We jump over all that stuff and look at everything from a higher level."

So let's examine this interaction. Clearly Sarah kicked your ass. You should work on that. Diving a little deeper:

1/ *"I'm the CMO for Omnitau. We make web apps."*
There are a few issues here. First, the name: *Omnitau* sounds totally made up. There are a few pleasing sounds and maybe an oblique reference to omnipotence but absolutely nothing to catch anyone's attention. The name is designed to go unnoticed—a bad idea for almost any new company. Also,

never say you make web apps. Web apps are rapidly approaching ubiquity. When you're introducing someone to what you do, why would you ever want it to sound uninteresting? Be sarcastic if you have to. No one is going to be interested in what you're doing if both your name, and the way you describe what you do, are yawn inducing.

2/ *"I work for Klipspringer."*
Klipspringer is an interesting word. It's a word that some people have heard of but probably can't place. This is a good thing. It fuels curiosity. Considering you're at a cloud expo, you would imagine there would be a lot of meteorological names: cloud this, cirrus that, cumulus something. So when everyone zigs like this, a name like *Klipspringer* zags. It sounds different which puts you in a position to show people why you're different. If your name sounds like everyone else's why should people believe you're not like everyone else?

3/ The payoff.

It's always good to reward people's curiosity. When you ask *"What's Klipspringer?"* there's a payoff—connecting the name to what you're doing in a cool way. Some great names make sense immediately. Those that elicit a question need to have a good answer. Creating the connection between the name and the positioning increases the likelihood people are going to remember your name and what you do. Your name should get a reaction, and a question is a great reaction. A question should lead you right into your pitch—so long as your name has a cool connection to what you're doing. This most likely has nothing to do with misspellings, dropped letters, and antiquated European languages.

Exercise 16
Take a few of your favorite names and jot down how they start to tell your story.

NAME

Field Exercise

Take a few of your favorite names and jot down how they start to tell your story.

NAME

142

NAME

Take a few of your favorite names and jot down how they start to tell your story.

NAME

NAME

The Proving Grounds
Do your names have the right stuff?

You're probably thinking, "*Awesome, we have a list of names, now let's pick our favorite.*" Wrong. Because of lawyers, you have a little more work to do.

1/ Look at all the names you've come up with. Highlight both the ones that are your favorites and the ones that do the best job of helping you tell your story.

2/ Google the names along with a few key-words for what your company does. So if you're an app development company search "*[name 1] app development building*" or whatever you think would yield results of relevant competition. If you find someone who does something in the same field as you with the same name, cross the name off the list. If you aren't sure, keep the name for now. This would also be a good time to check and see if your names mean "cobra sodomist" in Dutch or Korean [ahundred-monkeys. com/dcit]. Rinse and repeat for all your other highlighted names. You are going to submit the ones that pass inspection to an IP attorney for scrutiny, but you might as well save yourself a couple hundred bucks eliminating the options you know are taken.

3/ Legal

For as much as people focus on URL availability, it's a lot more important to make sure you do your homework in the trademark department. A URL can be changed relatively easily. A Cease and Desist, potential damages, plus finding and implementing a new name is a serious wrench in the gears no matter how you look at it. Thankfully, this is why trademark attorneys exist. You can typically get a preliminary report in the neighborhood of $50/name. You're going to need to give them a short description of the legal territory you want to cover.

The report should give you an idea of how available your potential names are. When you get down to your final three or four contenders, it's a good idea to run a more exhaustive search. This costs a little more money and takes a little more time, but it's a far better option than not knowing what's out there.

Just because you do a Google search and see some people using your name, doesn't necessarily mean you can't use it. As lawyers explain it to me, it's like a party: If you ring the door uninvited to a party and there's just a few people there, it's highly unlikely they're going to let you in. However if you show up to a party and the door is open, there's obnoxious techno blasting and a ton of people milling around, you might be able to get away with joining. So if there are just a few people with a trademark, they're probably going to want to protect it. If it's a crowded party, trademark ownership gets pretty complicated and people are less likely to defend their marks because they will probably have a harder time proving that you're invading their turf.

Considering I've never been to law school, I figured it would be a good idea to hear about trademarking names from an actual trademark attorney who works on this stuff everyday. So I sat down with Rebecca Liebowitz of *Venable LLP* in Washington D.C.

Who are you and what do you do?
I am Rebecca Liebowitz. I am a trademark attorney. I have been in the trademark field for about 18 years—started as a file clerk and a paralegal and I've had just about every title you could have. I have been a lawyer for about eight years. I focus largely on trademark clearance and prosecution—searching to see if trademarks are available, licensing and deals, purchasing trademarks, looking for potential issues.

Do I need to trademark my new name?
Yes.

Care to expound on that?
In the United States, trademark rights are established through filing or through use. If someone starts using a trademark, they don't actually need to register. However, filing a federal trademark gives you presumptive nationwide rights. In other words, even if you're only using your mark in southern California now, if you have a federal registration, you should be able to move into Florida easily. Common law rights (established through use) only apply to the geographic area where you're in business. So if you only have common law rights and are using it in southern California, that doesn't give you rights to use it in Florida. But if you have a federal registration you have presumptive nationwide rights and it freezes the rest of the country in terms of their existing use of that mark.

What if I plan to take my business worldwide?

Trademark rights are country-specific. And most countries are first to file rather than first to use meaning whomever files at the Trademark Office first can get superior rights. This means that it's important to have a strategy. It's very unlikely you will be able to file for everything, everywhere. Start with the countries and regions you're most likely to expand to and/or are notorious for trademark pirates.

How can so many companies use the same name?

Trademark rights are specific to the goods or services that you're using. *Delta Air Lines* and *Delta Faucet* is a good example. There's no likelihood of confusion because the goods/services offered by the two parties are completely different. Trademark rights are statutory and intended to protect the consumer. It means as a consumer you know the source of what you're buying.

Functionally, it breaks down into trademark classes. If you have a restaurant, you still may be able to stop someone from selling a barbecue sauce because those could be considered related goods. Consumers could expect a company to provide restaurant services and pre-made foods. Having a federal registration makes this easier to prove.

Can you do a brief overview of trademark classes?

The United States follows an international treaty. Most countries follow the same classification system. The system establishes 45 different classes. 1–34 are for products. 35–45 are for services. Generally the products within a class are lumped together based on their relatedness. For example, one class covers alcoholic beverages, excluding beer. Beer is categorized with non-alcoholic beverages. You have little-to-no control as a business owner over which class you fall into. Online, there is some wiggle room in terms of classification. For example, downloadable software is a product while online software is a service. Most countries accept really broad definitions of Goods & Services. The United States generally requires a higher level of specificity.

Can you still find yourself in trouble even if you're legally in the right?
Absolutely. Just like any other type of legal claim, just because someone alleges a wrongdoing, doesn't mean they are correct. There are "trademark bullies" that try to assert their trademark rights beyond that which they actually have—frequently against smaller companies. Or, you see smaller companies trying to do the same to larger companies who appear to have deep pockets. Unfortunately, until a mark has been registered for five years, a third party can challenge the registration owner's rights based on prior use.

What are the best types of trademarks?
Fanciful and Arbitrary Marks—these are

made-up words and existing words used completely out of context. "Apple" is not protectable for fruit, but it's very protectable for computers. Similarly, made up words like *Xerox* are very strong. From a marketing perspective, it takes a lot more time and money to get people to know it—escalator, thermos, trampoline—used to be trademarks. But over time their popularity turned them into generic words.

Suggestive Marks—these are marks that suggest something about the product or service but don't actually describe it. *Greyhound* for busses. Greyhounds are really fast dogs, so you assume the bus will be fast. *Coppertone* for suntan lotion is another suggestive mark. These names aren't as strong as Fanciful or Arbitrary Marks, but they're generally solid.

Descriptive Marks—these are the weakest. These are marks that describe the products/ services themselves or a characteristic of them. They're the hardest to protect because other people need to be able to describe what they do. If you've used a descriptive name for five-plus years and people have come to understand that designation as your product/service, you can strengthen your rights. Surnames and geographic indicators are also considered weak, although through extensive use (such as *McDonalds* for restaurants or *Hilton* for hotels) you can protect them.

Generic terms are not trademarks and not protectable—"Apple" for fruit, "Pencil" for writing instruments. In other words, if it's the common commercial name for an item, it is not a trademark.

What are things you can check on your own? You can search and access the USPTO database. It can be persnickety to use but you can find obvious conflicts pretty quickly. It can be complicated and esoteric, but it's a good place to start. The International

Trademark Association may be of use as well. (inta.org) Legal counsel can be helpful in understanding what actually constitutes consumer confusion. Marks don't need to be identical to create confusion.

Factors for likelihood of confusion include: similarity, relatedness of Goods & Services, similarity of channels of trade, conditions of purchase, how many other marks are out there on similar goods, and price point.

It is also useful to search the internet for your name with your intended Goods & Services. It can be easy to find conflicts this way.

How long does the registration process take? Can a name be safely used before the process is complete?
In the United States you can file on actual use or intent to use. In most cases you won't actually obtain a registration until you show use. How long it takes depends

on if you have use but generally speaking, an application filed based on use that doesn't encounter any problems will register in six-to-eight months.

What happens when you file an application?
You need to specify the Goods & Services on which you plan to use the mark. Within three-to-five months of filing the application, the Trademark Office will see if you meet all the basic requirements. If they have any issues, they issue what's called an Office Action. Then the applicant has six months to reply. You can either comply, modify or state your argument. If you're successful, the mark is approved and published for opposition. The mark remains open for 30 days for opposition by anyone who feels that they might be harmed by your registration. If it's not opposed, and the trademark is in use, a registration could issue within six-to-eight months. If it's based on intent to use the mark, a "notice of allowance" is issued and you have six months to

three years to begin to use the mark. If your application is based on your intent to use the mark, you stop the clock by filing the application, meaning that if someone else files after you, you still have the first shot at registration and once you obtain registration, your rights will date back to your filing date.

Heads Up

Trademark is only shades of gray—that is to say, there is almost no certainty to be had. It's just good to know who's out there and do what you can to avoid some trouble down the road. If you need help finding a trademark attorney, check out: ahundredmonkeys.com/dcit. Ask them to give you an example of a trademark report so you know what you're paying for. Usually they will rate preliminary results with an A–through–F or 1, 2, 3 grading system.

4/ After getting the trademark results back, assess your appetite for risk and select the passing names accordingly. Like I said, there's no "sure bets" in the trademark world so you should probably draw primarily from the "A" category unless you're unfazed by the threats presented for other names in the trademark report.

5/ Get down to some final contenders. The goal at this point is to have three to five names in contention.

If you have too many:
This is a good problem to have. Think about which names differentiate you the most from the competition. Think about which names get the biggest reaction out of people. Instead of asking them how they feel about a name, just say, *"I'm starting a [blank] called [blank]."* Don't ask. Just tell and gauge their reaction. A lot of people are really good at reading facial expressions and vocal intonation to see how you feel

about something before chiming in. Tell them the name with confidence, not like you're asking for permission. Writing out the answer to *"Why is your company called [blank]?"* can be helpful, too. If there's a strong connection and an interesting story, you're probably headed in the right direction.

If you have too few:

If you have too few names at this point, chances are the names you came up with are already taken. Go back to your big list of names and look into some of your more wild options. Revisit the *Types of Names* section and explore some more categories. Check out our lists resource here: ahundredmonkeys.com/dcit. Think of it as an excuse to be a little more daring.

If you're planning on registering for trademark, now is the time to take your best name(s) to a trademark attorney for registration.

Remember: while picking an interesting name might feel a little risky right now, six months down the road it won't feel like a risk at all. An interesting name is the best way to insure that the people who come in contact with your brand will remember you and want to engage with you. Boring and descriptive names are actually very risky because they don't make you think and are hard to remember. So please, don't take the risk of picking a boring name.

Back Matter

Eli Altman is Creative Director at the Berkeley, California-based naming company *A Hundred Monkeys*. He has led well over 400 naming projects from Silicon Valley startups to the products of Fortune 50 companies. He was responsible for developing the naming process at *A Hundred Monkeys* and previously at *MetaDesign*, San Francisco. Eli started naming before he stopped wearing Velcro shoes. He took his first paid naming job at 16. He calls Oakland, California, home.

@elialtman
@ahundredmonkeys

Back Matter

Colophon

DON'T CALL IT THAT
Eli Altman

ECP/003

©2016 Eli Altman
ahundredmonkeys.com

Design + Art Direction: Boon
boondesign.com

Editing: Marc Weidenbaum
dstl.info

Copy Editing: Eric Searleman

Lettering: Miguel Reyes
Commercial Type

Typography: Duplicate Sans + Ionic
commercialtype.com

Print Advisor: Celeste McMullin

Printed by Regal Printing Limited in HK

Second Edition: 1000

ISBN: 978–0–9898320–1–4

ExtraCurricular Press
This and other ExtraCurricular Press
printed matter can be ordered direct
from the publisher:
extracurricularpress.com

IMBROGLIO

NO PICNIC

STRAYS VOLTAGE

IZOLA

WIRE FOX

YOUNG Villains

* HYPERNYM *